TRIPS TO HEAVEN

RESURRECTION EXPERIENCE

RUTH MIRIAM DOW

To order additional copies of this book, contact:
Bookwhip
1-855-339-3589
https://www.bookwhip.com

CONTENTS

Introduction..vi

Part 1
E.F.'s Testimony

Chapter 1. The First Vision: The Beginning.................................3

Chapter 2. Death and Resurrection: 12-hour Trip to
Heaven and Hell...6

Chapter 3. The Second Vision - Fellowship with The Saints 29

Chapter 4. The Third Vision: Priesthood 32

Chapter 5. The Fourth Vision: God's Care for His Chosen Ones...37

Part 2
Monk Peter's Testimony

Chapter 6. The Life of Monk Peter of Saint Macarius 45

Chapter 7. A Sudden Call To Go 49
The Hour of Death 49
Two Great Opposing Powers: 50
The Robe..51

Chapter 8. Exit of the Spirit 52
Reactions To My Death..52
Time To Go...54
The Accusations..55
Critical Stage 56
The Door Is Closed 57

Chapter 9.   The Lamb Of God 58

   I Saw Jesus 58

   Sad Ending 59

   Mysteries of Heaven...60

   The Secret behind the Glimmer of the Threads of the Robe...................61

   The Blessed Virgin Mary..61

   The Loving and the Confessors 62

   Inheriting the Kingdom 63

Chapter 10. Back to Earth 64

INTRODUCTION

"**PART 1** of this Book contains four Visions, including the main Death and Resurrection experince. The true story of a young, illiterate, Coptic Christian man, who chose to remain anonymous except for his initials, lived in the Maghagha Province of El-Mynia, Upper Egypt in the early 1990's. Known only as "E. F.", he was married at the time, with one child. He had been hired by the Fourth-Century Monastery of St. Macarius during its renovation and expansion project, built according to the latest engineering standards, and embarked upon by its blessed Spiritual Abott, the departed Fr. Mathew the Poor (1914-2006).

"This account is not your typical Near-Death Experience (NDE), an increasingly-familiar, mainstream phenomena of the last 30 years, because the man clinically died for a full 12 hours. When 'Google-d', the longest-recorded and documented NDE was only 28 minutes long:

> 'Dannion Brinkley had an NDE that lasted 28 minutes. This is the longest, clinically-documented NDE ever recorded. His experiences during these 28 minutes are related in great detail in his wonderful and inspiring best seller "Saved by The Light".'

Clearly, this true story is unique in nature and unparalleled with any recorded Testimony in the last decades. No one prayed over E.F.'s dead body to bring him back to life; he was brought back by the Lord Jesus Christ Himself!

"This young man disclosed his story to his Spiritual Counselor, Father Elisha, one of the Elders of St. Macarius' Monastery, now deceased, who recorded it on a tape-recorder. He wrote that he knew E.F. personally, asserted the truth of his love for The Lord and His Church, being disciplined in Repentance, Confession and the receiving of The Holy Communion. The Father attributed E.F.'s many Visions to his simple and pure heart, quoting St. Isaac the Syrian:

> 'Divine revelations are typically given to those perfect Saints among us, because they are humble; for simple and pure hearts can neither be tempted by pride nor be puffed up.'

"Inspite of E.F.'s illiteracy, The Lord gave him Gifts to know and experience many Spiritual Mysteries. Since much of what he has seen in his Visions is supported by Biblical references - as well as the records, sayings and experiences of Church Saints - this is proof that these Visions are genuine, and gives them validity and valuable, Spiritual importance.

"What was so remarkable was The Lord's dealings with E.F. by these Visions, right after a fall or indiscretion, to encourage him to repent and return to Him – a personal Testimony to encourage us never to lose hope in The Lord's Mercy and His everlasting Love. An example in Scripture is the story of the Prodigal Son (Luke 15); and as He promised in the Book of Isaiah the Prophet:

> 'And now, thus says the Lord God who made you, O Jacob, and who formed you, O Israel: "Fear not, for I redeemed you. I called you by your name, for you are Mine. If you pass through water, I am with you; and the rivers shall not overflow you. If you pass through fire, you shall not be burned up, nor shall the flame consume you. For I am the Lord your God, the Holy One of Israel, who saves you. . . Since you were precious in My sight, you became glorious, and I love you. I will give many men for you and rulers to lead you."' *(Isaiah 43:1-4)

"The most prominent aspect of E.F.'s record is Chapter 2, in which E.F.'s spirit was snatched out of his body, and he was dead for almost 12 hours. During this time, he saw Heaven (Paradise) and firey Hell. He returned back to share all that he had seen, in great detail, revealing what our meeting with the Lord, the Great Judge, will be like:

> 'And if you call on the Father, **who without partiality judges according to each one's work**, conduct yourselves throughout the time of your stay here in fear;". *(1 Peter 1:17)

"**PART 2** is a hand-written account by a Monk, named Peter, of the Monastery of St. Macarius. Deceased on March 22nd, 1995, he wrote the detailed account of his former NDE by permission of his Guardian Angel. The Monks found the paper by his dead body, as they were alerted of his unexpected absence from Church Services.

"Now, we entrust you, Dear Reader, to the blessed E.F. and Monk Peter as they relay their personal Visions and experiences, with the hope of quickening your belief: '. . . in the things to come, for the time is short; for blessed are those who believe and have not seen'.

"May The Lord bless you as you seek to overcome all evil and share the reward: His Divinity, His Crown of Righteousness and His Home with us eternally - for which He sacrificed Himself.

Ruth Miriam Dow
Editor

PART 1

E.F.'S TESTIMONY

CHAPTER 1

THE FIRST VISION: THE BEGINNING

*"In the name of The Father, The Son, and
The Holy Spirit, One God, Amen."*

"Please accept my name as E.F. from the City of Maghagha, in the Province of El-Mynia, Egypt. What I know as being the beginning of The Lord's Dealings with me happened when I was tempted by my Cousin to join him in an illegal operation: a sinful act, indeed, in the sight of The Lord. Thousands of Egyptian Pounds (considered a huge sum of money at the time) was promised, if I agreed to work with him and his buddies in their evil scheme.

"I could not sleep that night, being torn and conflicted. On the one hand, in my heart, I knew that it was wrong to follow my Cousin's evil plot; but I could also imagine the fulfillment of all my dreams to get out of poverty, and my hopes for a better future. Suddenly, I saw a Vision that changed my entire life: the roof of my bedroom split wide open, and I was taken high above to a place full of light that surpassed the Sun's. I heard a very strong voice emanating from the middle of the light . . . The voice reverberated so loudly, as if it were being broadcast by multiple, hugh loudspeakers, filling all the corners of the sky.

"The Voice was of The Lord Jesus, who was sitting on a huge throne as King, with great honour and glory. He thundered in a stern and firm Voice:

> *'If you follow your Cousin in this scheme, you are not My Son, and I will disown you. You will go and will not come back . . . You will perish, and bring shame to My Name.'*

Later, I found myself back in my bedroom, and saw the Lord Jesus in a totally different appearance. Up in the Heavens, He was the King and Judge, full of great Glory; but the One in my room was very gentle, merciful and the Lover of mankind. In Heaven, He was rebuking me with an authoritative, very stern tone; but down here on Earth, He was counseling with an amazing Tenderness, Love and Compassion, urging me:

> *'Do not walk into this road, because it will lead to destruction . . . !'*

I said, 'Lord, you know what was tempting me is my need of money: poverty and lack of the basic necessities to build a home for my future family.' The Lord answered:

> *'Trust, Son . . . If you obey Me, I will ensure that you would never be in need of anything . . . I will grant you more than what you ask or even hope; but do not walk into this road. Be assured that your wicked Cousin, who tempted you, will receive his Judgement and be thrown into prison; and he will Eternally perish if he does not repent.'*

"My Cousin dropped by the next morning to pick me up and start the wicked adventure, as I had promised him; but I vehemently refused, without telling him what I had heard and seen. He repeatedly tried several temptations and rational persuasions, but found in me a resolute resistance as I turned him down. In the end, he went his way without me. The Lord's Words were literally fulfilled: my Cousin was arrested and received a 25-year, hard-labour prison sentence. I, on the other hand, was rescued - not only from a painful, Earthly punishment, but from an Eternal damnation: a punishment I would have deserved if it were not for the Lord's Love and Care.

"Before leaving me in this Vision, the Lord gave me a special, physical sign in my own body. I considered it a private and special "Grace", a sign of His perpetual Care and Protection: 'a single, long, silver hair He planted on my chest'. When the Vision ended and I awoke, I searched my body and was utterly surprised that it was not just a dream, and that I had received this Blessing, truly visible on my body. Immediately after this Vision, I began to experience Supernatural Powers, which were added to my natural body; and an amazing courage imbued my Soul, charging it with the audacity to undertake dangerous and high-risk challenges. The 'blessed hair' was a source of many material and Spriritual Blessings that I experienced at that time. The Lord told me:

> *'I will give you this Grace of a single hair, and I will take it away when you get married.'*

"And that is exactly what happened a few years later. The Lord appeared to me again, when I got married, to take away the single hair; but He said:

> *'I will give you a son in lieu of the single hair.'*

I was very sad to lose this 'single hair', because of the many Blessings I had received by its implantation on my body. The Lord comforted me when He found me weeping bitterly, and said:

> *'Do not weep. I will give the Grace of this single hair to your son, through whom I will perform many miraculous Works, in the future.'"*

CHAPTER 2

DEATH AND RESURRECTION: 12-HOUR TRIP TO HEAVEN AND HELL

1) A Trip to Heaven

"I got busy with family affairs and the cares of the world after my first encounter with the Lord; and yes, I admit, I acted foolishly in things common to man - and regrettably sinned. However, the Lord Jesus dealt with me differently this time, and in a more effective manner than the first time.

"One night, in late 1993, an Angel came and took me from my body. *(1) I had been asleep and stayed out of my body for approximately 12 hours: from 3:00 a.m. until between 3-4 p.m. the next day. Presumed to be clinically dead during this period, the house was gradually filled with relatives and neighbours, supporting my family, who did not stop weeping and wailing. In earnest, the Family started the funeral and burial arrangements, including the required permits; but The Lord was actively holding up such steps, making them ineffective; and the whole process, in essence, was delayed. In the meantime, members of my Family were dropping by, where my body laid on a bed: turning it and checking it again and again, at times they moved my body to a different room in the house. However, I could not feel a thing, because I was out of my body the whole time.

"As I was ascending, the features of my home, the street, the city, the country and then the Globe decreased in size; and then diminished before my eyes. I recognized the Angel accompanying me into the higher elevations of the stratosphere, where a satanic figure - a huge and horrific creature - approached me, and wanted to snatch me from the hands of the Angel. I was gripped with fear, holding tight to the Angel's hands and imploring: "Help . . . Please!". The satanic giant said to the Angel: 'This man belongs to us . . .', and started to enumerate the wicked evils I had done: 'He did so and so . . .' - one by one. Truly, he is the 'accuser against the brethren.' The Angel said: 'No, he belongs to us. I am in charge of guarding his Soul, and will not deliver him to you'. *(2)

"A fiery war erupted in the air between satan and my Guardian Angel, with swords of fire. I watched, fixated with fear, because of the ferocity and intensity of the fight. The battle was real, and I heard the clanking of swords clashing with such fierceness, as I watched from a cloud at the top of the battle scene. In the end, thank The Lord, the Angel won the battle; and I breathed a bit easier when the Angel warned satan:

'The Lord rebuke you . . . ! I am taking him with me, and will send him back to Earth by the Command of The Lord.'"

2) The Judgement of Souls before the Final One

"I saw, from afar, a gigantic Gate guarded by huge, dazzling Angels (they looked like Archangels) and other Angels of smaller stature, standing beside them. Having just departed from the world, a very long line-up of Souls stood in front of the closed Gate. I saw all Christian Souls bow down in worship, without exception, as they acknowledged the Lord Jesus Christ; but non-Christian Souls wept *(3). For all Souls, regardless of their belief or lack of it, instinctively knew, beyong any doubt, that Christ was The Lord and Judge of all.

"All Souls were naked. Judgement was given only to committed Christians, because all non-Christians and former Christians who denied their faith in Christ, go to their final destination without examination or Judgement - regardless of the excuses they offered. Not one had an acceptable excuse, reason or convincing evidence whereby he or she could not have put their trust in the Lord Jesus; so there is no need to go through an examination in Heaven, since they have been judged already on Earth, and their own consciences have witnessed against them. *(4)

"Examination in Heaven starts with an Angel carrying each Soul's 'Book of Life': a record of the good and evil deeds, accepted thoughts - even intentions - from the time the Soul is two years' old - or from the time it started to discern good from evil until its death. When the Angel reads what is written in the Soul's own Book of Life, one cannot estimate the time it takes to go over the whole life (regardless of its length). It feels like a twinkling of an eye to hear and acknowledge the details of everything in that life span (that extends up to even 120 years), because there is no time in Heaven. One knows that whatever the Angel reads is true, and every mouth will be silent because the records are so accurate and detailed. Then the Lord, the great King and Judge, thunders with one Statement from behind the closed Gate:

> *'Come in!'* or *'Welcome!'* to those whose good works triumphed over their evil doings; or *'Get out!'* to those whose evil doings eclipsed any goodness in their Books.

"A very tall, huge Angel, the size and height of Ramsis' Statue (moved recently to the Grand Egyptian Museum from Ramsis Square in Cairo) comes to each of these miserable Souls who heard their sentence to *'Get out!'*. He holds the poor Soul, tiny and insignificant like a small toy in his giant hands, and throws it into the unimaginable fiery Hell. However, for those Souls who have been granted to hear the welcoming voice, *'Come in!'*, the giant Gate opens immediately. First the Angels, assigned by the Lord, cover them with very shiny, white Robes, since no one can enter without being clothed with this radiant Robe, as described in Jesus' transfiguration:

> *'His clothes became shining, exceedingly white, like snow, such as no launderer on earth can whiten them.' *(Mark 9:3); and referred to in Mathew 17:1,2 and in John's Revelation 6:11, 3:4-5,7,9,14. *(5)*

Each Robe is custom-made to exactly fit the size of each Soul.

"While this was the general rule for good Souls, some righteous Souls, like the Souls of chosen bishops, priests, monks, nuns and laity, do not even have to wait in line for their examination *(6), and pass no judgement or condemnation. A great Angel directly ushers them in swiftly, no question asked:

> *'Open the gates; let the people enter who keep righteousness and guard the truth,'. *(Isaiah 26:2)*

"Yet there is another exceptional group of saintly Souls who have great stature and authority, and move in and out as if they own the place with the Lord Jesus. For example, when I was in the line-up awaiting my turn to be examined, I was terrified; so I prayed asking for the intercession of Pope Kyreles VI, (a Canonized Saint in the Coptic Orthodox Church, who passed away in 1970, and had been my Intercessor while I was on Earth). The Pope came out of the Gate to encourage me, assured me not to fear, and went back in as the giant Gate opened and closed to him automatically."

3) The Paradise of Joy - The Great Welcome

"When the departed Soul enters through the 'great Gate, after wearing the 'white Robe', it is welcomed by the Angels, Saints and the Righteous with great joy for their Salvation and in joining their Spiritual Family. *(7) Welcoming the Soul with an amazing embrace and outstanding affection, The Lord Jesus, Himself, hugs the Soul and puts His Hand around its shoulder in amazing Love and Friendship. No writer, orator or preacher can describe the depth of the tender Kindness and Love of Christ towards the Soul of man. In His Presence, the Soul feels that it knows The Lord from Eternity. Although I know this overwhelming Love, I find no human words capable of describing the all-sweet emotions which surpass all understanding. One does not want to leave Him, even for a single moment or the twinkling of an eye.

"Then The Lord leads every Soul to its own abode in Paradise. Yes, there are many mansions and different types of dwellings in the Father's Bosom in Paradise. Each place is a custom-made home that exactly fits each Soul, depending on its work. As The Lord leads the way, He starts to speak so gently to the Soul of its mistakes and omissions committed in the flesh: for example, being lazy in prayer, not being disciplined in Church Liturgical Worship, neglecting the partaking of the Holy Mysteries . . . Then The Lord speaks of virtues and good works, as if He were present with the Soul in the exact place and hour when they were done - as if He were living with the Soul moment-by-moment from the moment of its birth until its death.

"Upon arrival at the Soul's dwelling place, and as the Lord departs, the Soul feels sorry and a bit panicky that it will be apart from its Lover even for a moment; but it becomes surprisingly and quickly pleased as it sees The Lord, with His most-amazing, sweet Smile always before it, wherever the Soul moves from one place to the other."

4) My Abode in Paradise

"As for me personally, when the Lord welcomed me so warmly, full of love and compassion, He showed me the place that I deserved - and it was a poor, small and dark hut made of reeds. The Lord said:

> *'This is the place you deserve to stay in, because your good works are few and not complete before Me; however, look*

at this amazingly bright and great Palace. It is yours if you walk straight with integrity of heart, and produce fruits worthy of repentance; but if you neglect your righteous conduct, and your sins increase more than what you have committed so far, you will be deprived from entering my Paradise, and you will share the destiny of evil doers and non-Believers, who are cast out'.

He added:

'Scrutinize carefully this hut you deserve.'

"I went inside the hut and found a Book laid on a small table. I heard a Voice telling me:

'This is the Book that contains all your deeds, recorded every day of your life on Earth.'

The book was opened, and I saw different segments of writing: some were black, some were old, pale and almost erased. I was told:

'The black writings are sins and omissions that you have not repented of, but the ones erased have been confessed and repented of; because confession and repentance eradicate sins. *(8) However, the sins that you have confessed but are still holding onto in your heart, these sins, and your confessions of them, are both recorded, and will be eradicated only when you sincerely and completely repent of them.'

"Then I read in my Book of Life all the deeds and sayings, even the thoughts and intentions, good or bad, with a time-stamp recording the day and the hour, the time and place they happened."

5) In My Father's House are Many Dwellings:

"I also saw the other houses and mansions in Paradise. *(9) They were all different in shape, size, style and richness; each given depending on the worthiness of the Soul, in accordance with the faith and good works done. There were huge palaces, bright and full of glory, and others less lavish. There were two-storey homes and single-level ones; and yet I found Souls with no abode, sitting protected under a small hedge.

"I accompanied The Lord into a huge place made of all-crystal glass: the walls, ceiling and floor - of an indescribably magnificent Church, where the Saints were gathered. *(10) Since I was able to recognize each one as soon as I looked at their faces, I realized that the Soul has an immaculate ability to discern. Every one of the Saints had a special pillar in their name, where they can sit and read a Book (like a Bible). I was given a place to sit at the foot of one of those pillars, and was handed a similar Book. To my surprise, I was immediately able to read it with ease and fluency, in spite of being illiterate while on Earth. The Saints in this Heavenly Church joined the Angels in praising God with a language I did not remember, but I understood while there in Heaven.

"I saw many of the Saints, like the great Martyrs: St. George, St. Mina, St. Mercurius (also known by the name 'Abu-Seifein', which in Arabic means: 'The Holder of the Two Swords': Philopateer Mercurius), and Popes like Pope Kyreles VI. The Lord sends such great Saints down to Earth, on special assignments. They have authority from The Lord to go to any place on Earth, and return when they finish their duty. As for the married righteous Souls, they have delightful dwellings, and have freedom to move in Paradise; but they have no authority to descend to Earth like the other Saints.

"I noticed that St. George was the busiest and most-active among the special Saints on Earthly duties; and saw The Lord sending him often to help many - even non-Christians - who ask for his help. I heard The Lord tell St.George:

'Go down, Oh Hero. A lady named "Om (mother) Muhammad" needs your help and support'.

St. George went down, finished the job, came back in a few seconds, and bowed down to The Lord, telling Him of the healing he had performed on "Om Muhammad".

"Like a cuddled child, I asked the Lord: 'Lord, please give me The Communion (of Your Body and Blood)', since I did not partake of the Mysteries for approximately four years before my sudden death. The Lord Jesus brought me closer to Him; and He, the Master Himself - standing among all the Patriarchs and Bishops - put His Hand on my head, gave me the Absolution (the release and forgiveness of sins) *(11) and gave me His Body and Blood. *(12)"

6) Destiny of a Former Christian Who Abandoned the Faith of Christ

"Now, an incredible incident happened before my own eyes, during the Judgement of Souls that preceeded the hearing of the Lord's Voice, *'Welcome in!'* or *'Get out!'*. A former-Christian lady passed away at the same time as my departure; however, she had wickedly disowned Christ, denied the precious Faith in Him while she was on Earth, and had stayed in her denial until her death. As she heard the Voice, *'Get out!'* to receive her Eternal Judgment, the Virgin Mary, accompanied by Archangel Michael and St. George, came and took this lady to a room near the fiery Hell: the final abode of this miserable lady. I heard wailing and horrific crying reverberating from the room, as I saw the Virgin Mary coming out, holding the Body and Blood of Christ. The Body was shaped as the Communion Holy Bread, broken on the Holy Communion Paten; and the Blood, as the wine, in a small alabaster jar. The Archangel Michael held the jar of the Holy Myron (the Oil of the Holy Spirit used for Annointing and Confirmation); and finally, St. George held the Mystery Holy Oil of Healing the Sick and the Holy Water she either drank or which was sprinkled at her throughout her life in the Church. In other words, frightening as it sounds, this miserable lady was stripped from every Mystery of Grace she had received unworthily in her life. A dark, giant, demonic and very horrific figure came and viciously seized her, throwing her into the unbearable fire.

"As the wretched woman was about to be thrown, she saw the Lord Jesus from afar, and their eyes locked for a moment. Her eyes were full of sorrow and regret, and His eyes were full of pain and rebuke, because the time for repentance had passed. She understood, without words, all that the Lord was communicating to her.

"There are no spoken words in the spirit world; thoughts are transferred freely from one to the other. She understood that the time for repentance had passed, and she was not even worthy to keep any Spiritual Gifts or Mysteries she had received on Earth. Not only was she stripped of every good Gift, but she also would be thrown into eternal, fiery punishment. There is no harsher or more horrific punishment than that of the Soul who knew Christ, tasted the Heavenly Gifts and fell away from their Faith with no repentance or remorse, as they despised the Loving Lord (see Hebrews 6 and 10)."

7) Destiny of Saintly Clergy

"I saw the Souls of saintly Bishops as they departed from Earth. They came before The Lord, bowing down with great reverence; and He tenderly welcomed them, ushering then to their amazing abode, and said:

> 'This is your abode. Here, you are free to move around, and even visit your loved ones on Earth - total freedom; but this is your resting place.'

"When The Lord asks any of these Saints to serve on Earth, they are accompanied, the first time only, by an Angel in their descending; and in ascending when their Ministry is completed. After that, the Saints minister on Earth without the Angel's help."

8) The Destiny of the Righteous Laity

"As for the righteous laity and married people, they inherit their portion in Paradise and stay in their assigned dwellings *(13); but they do not have the additional freedom, given to the special group of Saints, mentioned earlier."

9) The Most-Excellent Group of Saints

"The Lord showed me all the various Angelic ranks: Archangels, Angels, Cherubim, Seraphim as well as the Prophets, Apostles, Martyrs, Confessors, Monks and Nuns. Each group sat in its row and place; but in the middle, the Lady Virgin Mother Mary sat on a great Throne, at the Right Hand of Christ Jesus, the Heavenly King and her Son.

"All the Saints welcomed me warmly; but the most affectionate with me was Pope Kyreles VI, since he was my private Intercessor on Earth. I was also able to immediately recognize others. For example: I had not known my Grandfather, for he had departed before I was born. Nevertheless, I immediately recognized him, and he warmly welcomed me. *(What a moment to be embraced by your loved ones in Heaven!)*

"In Heaven, I saw the most distinguished Saints burdened by their consuming love and concern for humans. Such Saints are entrusted with great Ministries to people on Earth. First, they always intercede before The Lord's Throne; then they go down to Earth to offer their amazing services to individuals and Churches alike. The most active, in this category, is the Virgin Mother St. Mary, followed by the great Martyr, St. George, whom The Lord constantly sends to Earth, more than any of the other Saints. Second in this class of 'Ministering Saints' are the Archangel Michael, the Martyr St. Mina, the Martyr Philopateer Mercurius and Pope Kyreles VI.

"Yet, there were other prominent Saints, like St. Shenouda the Archimandrite, with whom I was not acquainted when on Earth. I saw the Saint coming before the Throne of Christ, bowing down with great reverence and humility, then descending to Earth, wandering from Church to Church, offering help to many. He was also keen to nudge hearts, encouraging them to repent, showering them with numerous blessings.

"St. Shenouda introduced himself to me: he was quite tall, with a strikingly-bright and glorious face, so dignified, notably by a prominently-long beard as white as snow, wearing a hermit tunic with a hood and an embroidered, beautiful, golden cross."

10) The Judgment by The Lord Jesus Christ, The King

"As for the Lord Jesus Christ the King, Master and Judge of all, who can describe Him? There are no words to articulate His Beauty and Nature. He is so Gentle and Kind, never harsh. He does not condemn anyone, even evil doers; for His Heart bleeds sorrowfully as He sees them perish, and He leaves each Soul to judge itself on its own.

"Everyone, Christians and non-Christians alike, bow down prostrating at the huge Gate of Paradise as soon as they see the Lord Jesus, acknowledging Him as Lord, God and Judge of all. (Acts 2:36; Ephesians 1:21,22; 1 Timothy 5:20; 2 Timothy 4:1) If a person is a Christian, their Soul will pass through Judgment. Their own Book of Life is opened, and it receives what it deserves: either punishment or reward. But if the person is not a Christian, their Soul will be speechless, since it recognizes immediately that it has no excuse; for there is no need for this Soul to open its Book of Life and go through the Judgment. *(14) The Soul immediately judges itself, as it sees its unworthiness to be in Paradise, and to wear the Bridal white Robe, prepared only for the faithful among Believers. No one dares to protest that they are worthy to escape Hell on account of good works, no matter how great they are; for worthiness is not dependent on man-made good works, but on the living Faith in Christ Jesus, the Grace of Baptism and on the New Birth 'from Above', which culminates in a life in Christ, bearing fruits of righteousness.

"Similarly, the Christians who backslide and totally reject Faith in Christ, and die without repenting of their mortal sins, they sentence themselves to eternal damnation without the need to open their Books of Life or to go through Judgement. They are surrendered to a destination far worse than that of the non-Believer, after being stripped of every single Grace or Gift received on Earth.

"As for the Christians who believed in Christ, but died without receiving the Gift of Baptism: regardless of whether they were a child or older, they could not inherit and share the same heritage of the righteous Saints, even if they had good works. Yes, they do enter Paradise; but unfortunately, they dwell in a dark and dim place. They do feel the gracious state of the Saints: they hear their praise and sense their rapturous joy; yet they cannot have fellowship with them. While their abode is enveloped with darkness, they do not suffer pain or sorrow. They are in Paradise because of their Faith in Christ; yet deprived of the Baptismal Gift, they can feel the joys of the Saints, but cannot see any of it. (It appears there is a difference between entering Eternal Life and seeing Eternal Life. It is like a blind man: he can feel the warmth of the Sun, but cannot see its glory and light; he can smell the aroma of flowers and learn of their majestic colours and beauty, but cannot see any of them.

"Those who hear the Voice of The Lord: *'Come in!'*, hear an order without regret, for the Gate of Paradise is opened immediately for them by itself. The Angels put on them their assigned, custom-made, white Robes; they enter without fear of any retribution or concern for retreat.

They hear *'Congratulations! Congratulations!'* from the myriad of Saints, Angels and righteous Souls, then march in a procession dedicated for the Souls to be espoused to Christ, the Heavenly Bridegroom.

"As for me, I was praising The Lord with the Heavenly Choir in an atmosphere so intoxicating with sheer happiness, with an awareness of being unworthy of Christ's Gifts of overwhelming Peace and utter Joy that cannot be described, surpassing what the mind comprehends - for nothing on Earth resembles it. Therefore, I had no desire whatsoever to return back to Earth, for the whole world was so pitiful; and nothing in it can compare with the glory, radiance and perfect Love in Heaven. The Lord, however, willed that I return back to Earth to once more prepare for Heaven; but before my descent, the Lord wanted me to see Hell."

11) Visiting Hell

"When the sentence is announced to the Soul unworthy of Paradise and the Kingdom of Heaven, it hears the Lord's sorrowful Voice:

"Depart From Me!"

Convinced of the finality of the sentence, that carries no chance for appeal, the Soul raises no objection or argument; for no matter how good or righteous the person thinks they were while on Earth, everyone is resigned with certainty that **The Lord Christ alone** is the only righteous and just **Judge**, and that His Judgements are right and true.

"The Lord took me to see the 'abode of suffering' in fiery Hell. On approach, some distance away, I could feel the extreme heat-waves burning, blowing onto and scorching my face. I was shaken, and shrunk backward as a whiff of a lava-like wave hit me. The Lord held my hand and assured me that nothing would harm me, saying:

"This is the 'place of suffering' prepared only for satan and his angels. Sadly, however, they will be joined by those who choose, with their own free will, to join them in their wickedness and become evil doers or unbelievers or apostates."

I recognized some of my acquaintances and my relatives in-the-flesh. To my horror, I saw my own Grandmother immersed in fire, crying bitterly, calling me by name for help; and asking for anything that might relieve her pain. I had pity on her, and with an anguished heart, turned to the Lord pleading: *'Lord, she is my Grandma!'*. The Lord said:

'No one: not you, nor anyone else, can do anything for her; this is the place she deserves, for her deeds were evil.'

"As we continued, I observed various degrees and extents of fire covering each Soul in Hell, like that on a ladder. *(15) An extent of fire for one person may be limited to the feet only; another would go up as high as the waist; a third would totally immerse the Soul, even penetrate its inner organs. The gradual and granular measures of the fiery subjugation is proportional to the degree and severity of the evil deeds (committed and unrepented of), and to the state of each Soul. I also noticed an evil angel which rekindled the flame with its sword when the fire abated.

"I remember seeing people in Hell from every category and group: Laity, Monks, Priests - for indeed the Lord has no partiality. No one is great in His Sight, for He is the **Just and Truthful Judge**. I saw a great Bishop (like a Patriarch) wearing his stylish, priestly dress, totally immersed in fire. Every time he cried and tried to lift up his head, an angel hit him with a fiery sword, igniting the lava around and in him, extending his suffering even further. I was shocked and agonized over him, and I asked: *'Lord, why is such a great Bishop in Hell in the first place, and why is he suffering a great deal compared to others?'* The Lord answered:

*'This Bishop secretly denied me, in the time of persecution;
he worshipped idols, offering incense to them. When
persecution ended, he was restored to his Diocese, but offered
no repentance. I gave him three years to change by confessing
his sins, and sincerely repenting; but sadly, because of his
love of vainglory and fear of being dishonored, he ignored the
warnings and disregarded My loving Kindness and Patience.
Ultimately, he was taken, clothed with the garment of his sin
and denial, and received what he deserved.'*

"The Lord took me to visit other locations in Hell. One particular fiery spot was quite deep, oozing an awful smell that my nose could not bear - and has never experienced in my entire life. The dreadful stench was more horrific than that of dead dogs or people in their tombs. Later, I learned from The Lord that this was where Christians, who denied Christ, received their everlasting suffering, for their punishments were worse than that of non-Believers. I also saw the worms that never die: they were quite vicious with an unabated, ferocious appetite to eat anything they encountered. They were the size and length of great snakes, and they were not affected by the fire: unfazed by the unceasing scorch throughout the passing of time in Hell.

"There were other horrific sufferings in Hell, for which one would cringe in seeing them. What The Lord allowed me to see was limited and intended for me to change my behaviour: to quit, once and for all, my life of sin and disobedience against The Lord. He allowed it, not only for me to be spared the horrors of the fiery Hell, which I witnessed first-hand; but to offer the fruit of my repentance, and to be worthy of the Paradise I came to taste in its joy and ecstasy."

(Comment by the Translator: "St. Macarius asserts, in Sermon 36, that the degree of suffering and status of the Soul varies in Hell, similar to in Heaven; for as St. Paul states:

'There is one glory of the sun, another glory of the moon, and another glory of the stars; for one star differs from another star in glory.' *(1 Corinthians 15:41)

Likewise the sufferings in Hell vary according to evil deeds. He also states similar notions in Sermon 40.)

12) Return Back to Earth

"When my Guardian Angel took me up to Heaven, we faced a heavy battle from an angry demonic being: satan, the prince of the air, resisting my flight towards Paradise. Yet, on my way back down to Earth, it was **The Lord Jesus Himself** Who brought me back to inhabit my body; and there was absolutely no objection whatsoever from the demons or their prince.

"Twelve hours had passed when I returned to Earth. I landed back over a room in my home, where my dead body was laid. From the top of the ceiling, I saw my Parents and Siblings sitting around my dead body, weeping. My lifeless body was motionless, pitifully cold and stretched under a cotton-sheet covering. I realized then that I was still dead to them, as they were frantically endeavouring to finalize the purchase of my casket and burial plot.

"I recognized the apparent duality of my existence: the first was very much alive outside the body (my Soul that had not died) *(16); and the other (my physical body) was dead and laid on a couch. At this moment, the Lord Christ took hold of my Soul, and squeezed it into my dead body through my mouth, as if He was breathing my very existence back into my body. Immediately, I stretched and sat up, opening my eyes to the fright of everyone in the room.

"It took my Family several minutes to catch their breath, get out of the hysterical shock that froze their comprehension, and get used to me being alive again. Then my Father asked me - when I regained normalcy - his voice ironically mingled with brokenness and joy: 'Son, where were you? We were all very sad to lose you since we thought you were dead; we were about to bury you earlier, and at once, if it was not for an unforeseen complication in getting the Death Certificate . . .' I told him, along with the rest of the Family, my entire experience as it was fresh in my mind."

13) The World as Seen by Heaven's Inhabitants

"I would like to add one detail to that which was previously stated. While I was in Heaven, I was so surprised by the fact that Souls in Heaven know a great deal about us on Earth: I mean, the tiniest details. Everything here on Earth is seen, heard and known there in Heaven: we, to God and His Saints, are like an open book. I asked the Lord: how do they know? The Lord said:

'Come and see!'

The Lord showed me what appeared to be a spherical eye. When I looked through it, I was able to see everything with such clarity, sharpness, vivid details and colours - quite amazing indeed. I saw our planet Earth and its countries, cities, villages, homes, streets, and people - all kinds of people. I was able to distinctly see their faces and the expressions on each individual's face, with great accuracy. I was able to see my home, Family and to feel what my Father, Mother and Siblings were feeling in real time.

"As I scanned the Globe through this amazing lens or mirror, a very dark and awfully-smelly cloud like a thick, heavy smog, covered countries in their entirety. I observed that, as the cloud ascended to reach Heaven, its ugliness and stench were exponentially magnified. Then I understood that this fog represented the emissions from the shameful filth and unrestrained sinful practices committed by the people of these countries. This condition was accurately mentioned in the Bible several times, as in the case of the people before the flood:

'Then the Lord said, "The outcry against Sodom and Gomorrah has been completed, and their sins are exceedingly great.' *(Genesis 18:20);

and that of the city of Nineveh:

'Arise and go to Nineveh, the great city, and preach in it; for the cry of her wickedness has come up to Me.' *(Jonah 1:2)

"I was able to see and hear the slightest, miniscule detail of what happens on Earth, good and bad: both the abhorrently evil behaviours and the righteous, godly and loving deeds. I was given the ability to enter homes and see what happens inside, without being affected (in my Spirit) by the empty and vain practices of people on Earth. This state is a direct result of the Soul seeing the **Truth** in its strong affinity with the **Presence of God**; and the blessedness of Heavenly Life, as is described by St. Paul:

'For I am hard-pressed between the two, having a desire to depart and be with Christ, which is far better.' *(Philippians 1:23)

When I focused on one person, I was able to see the detailed life of this person, as if I were no more than five meters away. I saw many of my relatives, and the friends whom I used to mock: I had misjudged them to be overly-religious in going to Church regularly, and having a disciplined way-of-life, which lifestyle was actually imbued with the beautiful aroma of incense in Heaven."

14) Renewal and Change

"When I saw this, I repented of my entire, past way-of-life that had wasted away in the vanities of this world. I have determined to change my behaviour and life, for my Lord Christ Jesus showed me all this to reveal:

'And there is no creature hidden from His sight, but all things are naked and open to the eyes of Him to Whom we must give account.' *(Hebrews 4:13)

For the Lord knows everything inside our hearts. Even when He smells the hateful stench emanating from sinful Souls, The Lord is patiently waiting - out of His abundant, tender Mercies - for their awakening, to lead them to repentance, Salvation and His Kingdom. As St. Peter stated:

'The Lord is not slack concerning His promise, as some count slackness, but is longsuffering toward us, not willing that any should perish but that all should come to repentance.' *** (2 Peter 3:9)**

"To Him, the Lord Jesus Christ, be glory, with His good Father and the Holy Spirit, now and forever more, and to the end of the ages.

"Amen."

<u>Chapter 2 Footnotes (*)</u>

1. Church Fathers confirmed the truth about the existance of a Guardian Angel for every Christian Believer. (Examples: St.Macarius The Great, Sermon 22; St. Isaac the Syrian, Volume 1, M. 5; St. Shenouda's Sermons during the Holy Week of Pascha). St. Macarius states specifically that the Guardian Angels receive the righteous Souls and carry them to their assigned habitation.

    [Added by the Translator: *"So it was that the beggar died, and was carried by the angels to Abraham's bosom. The rich man also died and was buried." *(Luke 16:22)*]

2. St. Anthony's Biography, written by St. Athanasius of Alexandria, mentions a Vison where the Saint saw a huge giant - horrible, fierce and cruel - standing in the way of the Souls ascending after death. St. Anthony was told that the identity of this giant was satan himself, who attempts to stop and arrest every Soul that belonges to him; but he could not succeed in stopping the Souls of the righteous Ones.

3. This is what The Lord Jesus said: *"Then the sign of the Son of Man will appear in heaven, and then all the tribes of the earth will mourn, and they will see the Son of Man coming on the clouds of heaven with power and great glory." *(Mathew 24:30)*

4. The Lord Jesus said: *"He who believes in Him is not condemned; but he who does not believe is condemned already, because he has not believed in the name of the only begotten Son of God." *(John 3:18)*

5. *"Then a white robe was given to each of them;".* *(Revelaion 6: 11)

6. This is a confirmation of the Lord's saying: *"Most assuredly, I say to you, he who hears My word and believes in Him who sent*

Me has everlasting life, and shall not come into judgment, but has passed from death into life." *(John 5:24).

Further, by St. Paul: *"There is* therefore now no condemnation to those who are in Christ Jesus, who *do not walk according to the flesh, but according to the Spirit." *(Romans 8:1)*

7. The Soul truly becomes as described by St. Paul: *"Now, therefore, you are no longer strangers and foreigners, but fellow citizens with the saints and members of the household of God, . . ." *(Ephesians 2:19)*

8. As St. John attests in his Epistle: *"If we confess our sins, He is faithful and just to forgive us our* sins and to cleanse us from all unrighteousness." *(1 John 1:9).*

   Also Isaiah the Prophet says: *"I, even* I, *am* He w*ho blots out your lawlessness, and I will not remember them." *(Isaiah 43:25)*

9. The Lord stresses this fact: *"In My Father's house are many mansions; if it were* not *so,* I would have told you. I go to prepare a place for you." *(John 14:2)*

10. As described: *"The foundations of the wall of the city were* adorned with all kinds of precious stones: *the first foundation was jasper, the second sapphire, the third chalcedony, the fourth emerald . . . " *(Revelation 21:19)*

11. The Church truly belives that the Lord Himself is the one who gives the Absolution to the congregation by the mouth of the Priest, as stated in the Liturgical Absolution prayer to the Father: *"Remember, O Lord, my own weakness, and forgive my many sins; and where transgression has abounded, let Your Grace be multiplied in abundance. Because of my own sins and the abomination of my heart, deprive not Your people of the Grace of Your Holy Spirit. Absolve us, and absolve all Your people from every sin, from every curse, from every denial, from every false oath, and from every encounter with the heretics and the heathens."*

12. The Church also believes that the Lord Himself is the one who gives His people of His Own most Holy Body and Blood through the Priest. This will be expounded further in Chapter 4.

13. As St. Macarius the Egyptian said in Homily #36: *"As in a city there are multitudes of people, and some are infant children, some men, or young men; but all drink water of one well, and all eat of one bread, and have one air to breathe; or as lamps are: one with two wicks and one with seven; but where the greater abundance of light is, the illumination is greater. So, as many as are in fire and light cannot be in darkness; but there is much difference. If a father has two sons, one a child, the other a young man, he sends the one abroad to foreign cities and countries; but the little one, he keeps continually under guard, because he can do nothing."*

14. This is what the Lord said: ***"Jesus answered, 'Most assuredly, I say to you, unless one is born of water and the Spirit, he cannot enter the kingdom of God.'"*** *(John 3:5)*. And also: ***"He who believes and is baptized will be saved; but he who does not believe will be condemned."*** *(Mark 16:16)*

15. St. Macarius the Egyptian asserts, in Sermon 36, that the degree of suffering and status of the Soul varies in Hell, similar to the variety of degrees of glory experienced by the Saints in Heaven; for as St. Paul states: ***"There is one glory of the sun, another glory of the moon, and another glory of the stars; for one star differs from another star in glory."*** *(1 Corinthians 15:41)*

Likewise, the sufferings in Hell vary according to evil deeds. He also states similar notions in Sermon 40: *"In light and glory, there are differences, and in hell itself; and punishment appears poisoners and robbers, as well as others who have committed only little sins. Those who say that there is one Kingdom and one hell, and that there are no degrees, say ill."*

16. As St. Macarius the Egyptian said in Homily #7: *"For this body is a similitude of the Soul, and the Soul is the image of the Spirit; and*

as the body without the Soul is dead, and unable to do anything at all; so without the heavenly Soul, that is, without the Divine Spirit, the Soul is dead from the Kingdom, being unable to do any of the things of God without the Spirit". Also in Homily #30: *"For as in the world, the Soul is the life of the body; so in the Eternal Heavenly World, the life of the Soul is the Spirit of the Godhead. Without the life of the Spirit, this Soul is dead to those above, and of no use."* He also asserts in Homily #2, that the Soul has corresponding senses to those in the body: *"We have put on the new and Heavenly man, Jesus Christ, once more corresponding: eyes to eyes, ears to ears, head to head - to be all pure, and wearing the Heavenly image."*

CHAPTER 3

THE SECOND VISION - FELLOWSHIP WITH THE SAINTS

"I got drafted into the Egyptian army years after my Death and Resurrection experience. Far away from inhabitants, my army regiment was stationed in a remote, isolated mountain area. One night, I was on my assigned watch that started at 2:00 a.m. After having a bit of bread and feta cheese, I got up to start my duty. Part of my watch was to regularly circle the camp. I then heard constant Church bells ringing melodically. Intrigued and surprised, I walked steadily toward the sound that was beaming from the top of the nearby hill. As I became increasingly drawn to it, I looked at my watch, and it stood between 2:30 to 3:00 a.m. Then I heard an overpowering melody, a complete night praise-worship chanted by Saintly Spirits. I used to listen and participate in similar night praise-worships in monasteries. From their amazing, harmonious voices, I concluded that they were a huge crowd singing with one voice. I heard the complete praise-service but saw no one.

"The Choir started to pray the Matins, and I smelled the aroma of incense; then I heard a complete Liturgy, that ended with Communion. I was happily mesmerized throughout the prayer, as if I was transformed to a different world, and could not feel the passing of time. At the end

29

of the Mass, a white hand was extended to me, and showered me with Holy Water, drenching my coverall. I then heard a voice telling me:

"Go in peace; the Peace of the Lord be with you."

"I regretted eating earlier, as normally I fasted before partaking of Communion; and therefore understood why the Holy Mysteries were not offered to me. When I checked my watch, it was 6:00 a.m. More than three-and-a-half hours had passed like the twinkling-of-an-eye, as I felt raptured with this Heavenly Church Choir."

An Earlier Vision

"I would like to mention that, before knowing the Lord and my death experience, in which I saw Paradise and Hell, I was a foolish young man, behaving in a selfish, rotten way. My father used to force me, against my will, to go to Church; and he used the rod, at times, because of my stubbornness and refusal to obey; but this increased my disdain and mockery, for I used to say:

'What is the benefit of going to Church? What is the Church, anyway?'

"One day, I reluctantly went to attend the Liturgy, and stood in a Church pew aimlessly, with the same careless disdain. Suddenly, I saw Three People inside the altar, alongside the serving Priest and Deacons, having such radiant faces and white Robes. One of the Three was carrying a fiery Sword. I saw a radiant Hand of an Invisible Person extending over the Mysteries on the Altar, blessing the Oblations to become the Body and Blood of Christ.

"I told the serving Priest what I saw after the Liturgy was over, and he smiled saying:

'Son, do not mention this to anyone. The extended Hand that blesses and transforms the Oblations into Christ's Body and Blood is the Hand of the Lord Himself. As for Three radiant People, they are the Angels of the Altar and of the Oblations. By the way, the departed Pope Kyreles VI attended the Liturgy as well with us.'

"It was an amazing Liturgy that left a big impact on my life. From that day forward, I knew the mystery of the Church: The Mystical Body of Christ, hidden from the world as it was hidden from me and from many others, exactly as St. Paul explained:

"But we speak the wisdom of God in a mystery, the hidden wisdom which God ordained before the ages for our glory, which none of the rulers of this age knew; for had they known, they would not have crucified the Lord of glory." (1 Corinthians 2:7,8)

CHAPTER 4

THE THIRD VISION: PRIESTHOOD

"For such a High Priest (Jesus) was fitting for us, who is holy, harmless, undefiled, separate from sinners, and has become higher than the heavens,". *(Hebrews 7:26)

"I was offended, one day, by one of the Priests serving in my Village Church, where I prayed and served regularly. This Priest happened to also be my 'Father in Confession'. The offence had to do with a wrong behaviour, committed by the Priest, against others and myself. Out of love for him, and following the Biblical standard as The Lord taught us, I approached Him to present the matter to his attention, and hopefully prevent any reoccurrence of the offense. Unfortunately, not only did the Priest not accept my appeal, but he also punished me by forbidding me to have Communion.

"I went to pray the Church Liturgy that day with a broken heart. I was sad to the point that I had decided not to offer the priest forgiveness when he asked for it, during the Liturgy, before he prayed the 'Reconciliation Prayer': when the Priest would customarily kneel down and ask:

'Forgive me fathers and brothers, for I have sinned',

I planned to respond out loud:

'I do not forgive you!'

This way, I intended to stop him from completing the Liturgy. But the Lord miraculously prevented me, and He comforted my Soul with a Vision revealing that if one of His Servants was unfaithful over the Master's Flock, the Lord would continue to be forever faithful.

"I saw, at the beginning of the Liturgy - as the Priest started to choose one of the 'Korban' breads - two Hands of an 'Invisible Person' appear, and hold the Priest's hands in chains. They were kept tied up by his side. From this time onward and until the end of the Liturgy, the two Hands of the "Invisible Person" were in charge, lifting up in prayer, blessing and performing all Liturgical Services.

"I looked closely, from the side Altar, at the time of the 'Remembrance of Saints Prayer', and realized that the serving Priest's hands were still tied in chains. The other two Hands were the Ones blessing the consecrated Bread and Holy Chalice. I was greatly moved by the Vision, and desired to receive the Holy Mysteries. Remembering the Priest's Excommunication of me, I was conflicted. I reasoned that perhaps I should ask him first for an 'Absolution'; but I was so reluctant, concerned he might kick me out when he saw me. Tossed around, back and forth in my mind, my conscience was torn apart. However, I became so encouraged, seeing the Altar suddenly engulfed by Hosts of Saints wearing glorious white Robes, and standing in such amazing awe and reverence. In fact, I saw the face of each one enlarged as their respective name was mentioned audibly in the 'Commemoration of the Saints Litany'.

"When I approached the Altar, I saw the bright 'Being' of the two, radiant Hands: He was the One who put His Hands on my head, prayed for me to be absolved and handed me the Holy Body and the precious Blood. He also gave the Congregants - except a few - His blessed Mysteries, looking sadly and grieved over the few from whom He withheld His Gifts. Frozen in their seats, they did not dare to approach

Communion after His Rebuke. The Heavenly Vision came to an end as soon as the Liturgy was over, right after the Communion and the showering of the congregation with Holy Water. The Lord, along with His Heavenly Angels and Saints, then disappeared. Looking extremely tired, frail and sad, I saw that the serving Priest's hands were loosened.

"I understood that the Lord's Intent from this Vision was to comfort my heart, and teach me that I should take no offense over the Mystery of Priesthood or the sanctity and validity of the rest of the Church Sacraments when the serving Priest is out-of-line and sinning; for these Sacraments are not established on the basis of goodness or righteousness of the Priest, but on the Lord Jesus Christ Himself. Furthermore, the efficacy of the Grace in these Holy Sacraments cannot be nulled or emptied-out because of the Priest's weakness or error; for the Sacraments are based on the Living Faith in Christ, who Himself performs them as our Holy and undefiled High Priest.

(Footnote by the original Author: "E.F., the Seer of this Vision, did not know this Truth from reading books or human teaching, for he confessed that he was an illiterate man. His Vision, however, reflects and confirms the Early Fathers' teaching on Priesthood, as St. John Chrysostom has said:

> 'The hands are laid on the head of the 'ordained man' (to become Priest), so that God can do everything through him.'

St. John Chrysostom also said:

> 'The Lord, who reclined in the Last Supper, is the One who is reclining now, in His Temple and around His Altar/Table; for Jesus Christ is yesterday, today, and forever; for no human (Priest) transforms the bread and wine making them The Lord's Own Body and Blood. Therefore, when you see a human Priest giving you the 'Holy Body (and the precious Blood)', believe that you're receiving them from the Lord Himself. Similarly, in Baptism (or

any other Sacrament you receive), believe that no man, an angel or archangel, is capable or dares to approach you to impart these life-giving Mysteries but the Lord Himself. For the 'Gift' is the Lord's alone; for since He is the One who offered Himself on our behalf as a Sacrifice on the Cross, He is the only One worthy to offer His Body and Blood by Himself.' (John Crysostom on Sacraments Homily #50).

"From this understanding, our saintly early Bishops and Fathers always looked at themselves as only stewards in serving their Master, The 'Great Shepherd'.

> **'Shepherd the flock of God which is among you, serving as overseers, not by compulsion but willingly, not for dishonest gain but eagerly; nor as being lords over those entrusted to you, but being examples to the flock; and when the Chief Shepherd appears, you will receive the crown of glory that does not fade away.' *(1 Peter 5:2-4)**

"Furthermore, the Bishops, along with the rest of the Clergy, considered themselves among the sheep and needed, like the rest of the flock, the care of the 'Great Shepherd', as St. Augustine, the Bishop of Hippo, said to his flock:

> *'We watchguard over your Souls as good stewards to God, but at the same time, we look at Him to guard us as well. For if we were like shepherds to you, yet we are in need to be shepherded by God; for we are, with you, lambs of the Good Shepherd. Let us be humble, not thinking highly of ourselves, for nothing good is in us that we did not receive from 'The Only Good One'.*

As the Lord Jesus said:

> **'. . . Why do you call Me good? No one is good but One, that is, God.' *(Luke 18:19)**

"When the fourth-century Monk and 'Father of Ekonomia' (Greek for Fellowship) met and saw his Disciple Tadros for the first time, standing at the door weeping, St. Pachomius welcomed him in fear and trembling, saying in great humility:

'Do not cry my son, for I am Your Father's servant'.

"All these, and other great fathers, considered themselves only bond slaves, serving the Children of the Living Lord in word and deed, obeying His commandment as in:

> *'Yet it shall not be so among you; but whoever desires to become great among you shall be your servant. And whoever of you desires to be first shall be slave of all. For even the Son of Man did not come to be served, but to serve, and to give His life a ransom for many.' *(Mark 10:43-45)*

> *'But not so among you; on the contrary, he who is greatest among you, let him be as the younger, and he who governs as he who serves. For who is greater, he who sits at the table, or he who serves? Is it not he who sits at the table? Yet I am among you as the One who serves.' *(Luke 22:26, 27)*

> *'And He sat down, called the twelve, and said to them, "If anyone desires to be first, he shall be last of all and servant of all.' *(Mark 9:35)*

CHAPTER 5

THE FOURTH VISION: GOD'S CARE FOR HIS CHOSEN ONES

"He who dwells in the help of the Most High

Shall lodge in the shelter of the God of heaven.

He shall say to the Lord, 'You are my protector and my refuge,

My God; I will hope in Him;

For He shall free me from the snare of the hunters,

And from every troubling word.'

He shall overshadow you with His shoulders,

And under His wings you shall hope;

His truth shall encircle you with a shield." *(Psalm 91:1-4)

". . . He encircled him; He instructed him; He guarded him carefully as the apple of His eye." *(Deuteronomy 32:10)

"When I was enscripted in the Egyptian Army Corps of Engineers, I joined my Battalion on an assignment to one of the Military Air Bases, located somewhere off the Cairo-Alexandrian Desert Highway. The Assignment's mandate was focused on the removal of landmines -remnants left from WWII. My group camped in one of the tents we errected, just outside the landmine field's barbed fence, in the middle of a totally uninhabited desert.

"When we settled down, I went for my usual prayer walk. Lifting up my eyes to the Heavens and a beautiful blue sky, I started: "Our Father who art in Heaven . . ." I reached a remote spot, and thought that it would be a perfect, private place to pray and commune with my beloved Lord, without any interruption. As I entered this private spot, it was surrounded by a barbed wire, and there was a sign with words that I did not understand. I was totally oblivious to the great danger of stepping into this area, because I was illiterate - unable to read or write. Later I was told that the sign had the following warning words: 'DEADLY DANGER!!! Do not come close. Landmine.'

"I simply did not give any attention to the sign or the warning words, and went in to pray. By the way, I do not know how to pray, other than the Lord's prayer: 'Our Father . . .', and some songs and Kyrilaison (Lord have mercy), along with some memorized portions of the Coptic Liturgy. Later on, I found out that this spot was right in the middle of the landmine field that we were assigned to clear.

"Apparently, the Commander of my Battalion was watching me, using his binoculars from a high hill outside the field; but since I was totally engrossed in my worship, praying and singing, I was unaware of either the danger around me or of the Commander's watchful and probing eyes. I kept on walking, totally absorbed in my prayers, with my eyes fixated on Heaven, unintentionally stepping on the landmines as if I was in a beautiful garden, crossing myself with the Holy Cross, and praying 'Our Father . . .' Suddenly, I saw and heard the mines exploding around me, and the sharpnels flying everywhere. I was so perplexed since, amazingly, nothing was touching me.

"I looked underneath me to find a huge 'Hand' full of Light, with a stretched-out Arm extended, carrying me and literally encamping me.

Inside the Divine 'Hand', I was like the nut inside the nutcracker. In shock, I was in awe of this amazing Vision. Kneeling down, leaning on the inner wall of the Divine 'Hand', I was totally protected and submersed in peace and serenity. It was the mighty 'Hand of God'.

(Footnote of original Author: "The Holy Scriptures identify Christ the Lord and Son of God as the Mighty Hand of God, like in Exodus 13:3, 14, and similar Scriptures:

> *'Then Moses said to the people, "Remember this day, in which you went out from the land of Egypt, out of the house of bondage; for by strength of hand the Lord brought you out fom this place. No leavened bread shall be eaten."' *(Exodus 13:3)*

> *'So it shall be, when your son asks you in time to come, saying, "What is this?" that you shall say to him, "With a strong hand, the Lord brought us out of Egypt, out of the house of bondage".' *(Exodus 13:14)*

> *'Send forth Your hand from on high; deliver me and save me from great waters, from the hand of the sons of foreigners,'. *(Psalm 144:7)*

> *'I looked, but there was no helper; and I observed, but there was no one to help; therefore, My arm delivered them, and My anger was suddenly present.' *(Isaiah 63:5))*

"I was watching and hearing the hellish, fiery explosions with amazement, as I was sitting inside this mighty Hand. Driving his Jeep, the Commander of the Battalion rushed, as close as safely possible, to my position. He called with a loud voice, commanding me to get out of the area immediately. (He must have been cursing me for my stupid action). Following the Order, I walked out without a scratch. The Commander was dumbfounded and utterly speechless, since he found me not only safe and sound, but walking out with a clean coverall: no smudge of a smoke or burn stain.

"What is your name?", the Captain demanded. When I answered, he knew that I was a Christain, so he added: 'And Christian too?' He meant that I not only commited a crime by entering a forbidden area, but also by being a Christian. However, I was not afraid of his words or threats. When he saw me quite unperturbed, he shouted angrily: 'How on earth are you not dead?'

"He examined my body to ensure that I was whole, and there were no injuries. I could not answer at first, thinking to myself: 'How could I explain what happened to an unbeliever?' The Captain threatened me then: 'I want to know the truth; otherwise, I will lock you down immediately in the camp's jail.' I answered: 'I beg your pardon, Captain, because I am nothing: it is the Lord Jesus Christ, my Master, who delivered and rescued me.' So he asked: 'What did He do?' I said: 'The Lord put me in His Hand, and covered all of me, shielding me from the landmines exploding around me.' The Captain then shouted, challenging me: 'Okay, come on then right now; we will enter the field together to make sure that what you said is true.' Without any hesitation or a hint of fear, I answered: 'Certainly!' The Captain fetched from his jeep the 'landmine detection equipment', and we walked. I was in the front, walking fearlessly, with no protection or detection device, and he was behind me. He was astounded by my courage and asked me: 'Aren't you afraid of death?' Full of the Holy Spirit and Faith, I answered: 'The One Who protected me from landmines and death, in my entrance and exit the first time, is able to protect now, any time and everywhere; for He is a refuge and strong fortress to those who lean on Him.'

"Hesitantly, the Captain followed my footsteps, consciously and deliberately feeling out every single trigger or cracking sound emitted from the equipment in his hands. Walking slowly, he moved up to a point, then called me to stop. This was the location where he first saw me. Although he had not seen me inside the stretched, huge Hand, the Captain was able to see clearly the vivid imprint of the 'Hand' on the sand, while all the remnant of the shrapnels from the exploded mines stood outside and around the spot where the Hand acted like an impregnable shield.

"Few minutes had passed as if it were a lifetime; the Captain stayed silent in a state of shock and bewilderment. Overwhelmed with emotions, he knelt down, kissing the sand. Uncontrollably weeping with a loud voice, he said repeatedly, 'Forgive me, Jesus of the Nassara (a name used by Muslims in the Middle East to degrade Christians; it means those who belong to the Nazarene). I tried, with no avail, to quieten my Captain, since he was gripped with overwhelming grief for his misjudgement of me and my Lord. He continued to ask forgiveness from the Lord Jesus, and from me, for the insults and mistreatment that he had lashed out at me.

"The Captain ordered the building of a cement wall around this spot, and forbade anyone from treading on it. As a blessing from the Holy spot, where the 'Hand' was visible, he took a bag full of sand for his Family and relatives. He asked me if I carried anything Holy as a blessing, so I gave him my pocket-sized Bible that I used to carry on me all the time.

"The Captain was not a Christian: until this incident, he used to live by the spirit of this world, going after his lust and ambition to the extreme. Furthermore, he was rude, harsh and aggressive, exceeding his military disposition. Yet, praise be to God, this incident completely changed his life. He became chaste, content, meek and loving to everyone around him, with no hint of partiality or discrimenation.

"Gradually, the Captain started to show his hunger to know the Truth of the Mysteries of the Gospel. Many times I could not directly answer him, because I did not know; but I was able to immediately lift my face to Heaven and pray that the Lord would provide me with the suitable answer - and He always did. My answers were at a Spiritual level that exceeded my tiny, illiterate mind and my simple comprehension of things; for The Lord was fulfilling His promise to teach the meek and humble His ways:

> *'He will guide the gentle in judgment; He will teach the gentle His ways.' *(Psalm 25:9)*

Further, it was for the glory of God Himself:

> *'But sanctify the Lord God in your hearts, and always be ready to give a defense to everyone who asks you a reason for the hope that is in you, with meekness and fear.' *(1 Peter 3:15)*

"Later on, the Grace of the Lord touched the Captain, securing him and all his family as they turned, putting their faith in Christ alone. Glory and honor be to Him forever!!!"

PART 2

MONK PETER'S TESTIMONY

CHAPTER 1

THE LIFE OF MONK PETER OF SAINT MACARIUS

"Monk Peter was born on December 9, 1950, to a righteous and well-to-do family in Cairo, Egypt. Named Kamel by his parents, meaning 'Perfect' in Arabic, he excelled in his studies and graduated from High School. His father took him to the late Pope Kyreles for a blessing and advice. Startled by the Pope's predictions, which indicated that Kamel would be an engineer first and later become a Monk, these words became prophetic when Kamel finished top of his 1973 Class, and was assigned to be a teacher of Mechanical Engineering at the University of Ein-Shams in Cairo.

"During his university years and right after graduation, Kamel used to frequently visit the 4th-Century St. Macarius Monastery; and as a result, the love of Christ grew tenderly in his heart. He heard the Lord's Divine Call to the monastic life on one of his visits, as he was praying the Prime Early-morning Psalms, specifically:

> *"Listen, O daughter, behold and incline your ear, and forget your people and your father's house; for the King desired your beauty, for He is your Lord." *(Psalm 45:11,12)*

The words penetrated his heart, and he intuitively knew that the Spirit was talking to him personally with these words. In spite of the vicious fight of the enemy to dissuade him from the Holy Call, he determined to obey the Lord's Voice and wrote his letter of resignation.

"A combination of insidious temptations and serious Family bonds and obligations became obstacles; only one was more than enough to prevent, or at least delay, his farewell to the world and become a novice Monk. During this decisive period, he was offered a very lucrative position, a marriage to a very-wealthy young lady, and an Immigration Visa to Canada. But the most painful hurdle was the death of his father, leaving his widowed Mother and two young Sisters for him to look after. When Father Mathew-the-Poor knew his family conditions, he felt for the family left behind; and suggested that he could return to his family until the Lord opened the door. Miraculously, his family was supportive of his decision for the Angelic life, and the elder Sister got engaged. Evidently, The Lord was giving him the green light, and confirming that he should not worry; because The Lord Himself would take care of them.

"Kamel took the name Peter when ordained a Monk on the 25th of August, 1975. An amazing love story with The Lord lasted 20 years on Earth, to be consummated in Eternity. From the first day of his Call, Monk Peter knew how to 'die to self' serving others, fulfilling the vow of true poverty, and offering all his knowledge and exceptional intelligence to every one of his monastic Brothers and Fathers. He was assigned to manage the maintenance of the Monastery's heavy equipment, used in the construction-upgrade project: excavators, backhoes, bulldozers, loaders, trucks and others. Always with a beautiful smile, he worked hard with his other Brother Monks and the hired workers alike.

"Monk Peter left his fingerprint on most of the Monastery's projects, directly or indirectly. For example, he was the final Engineering Consultant to recommend pursuing the purchase of new equipment or executing a task. He designed and executed a silos-and-dehydrators project to preserve the agriculture and fruit produce from being ruined until they were distributed. For the chicken farm, he designed the electrical network. He participated in all the technical aspects of the Monastery Land on the Mediterranian Sea, requiring him to travel extensively outside the Monastery, inside Egypt and abroad: mostly to Western Europe including Germany, France, Britain, Spain and Italy to acquire the Monastery's needs for heavy equipment, agriculture seeds and fertilizers. During the last 16 years of his life, he calculated that the number of kilometers he had personally travelled added up to half the diameter of the entire Globe.

"Everyone who encountered Monk Peter has witnessed that 'they have seen the Work of God and Saint Macarius in this gentle Monk'. The Lord used him to save many Souls and families from breakdown. A peacemaker, he could not bare to see two of his monastic Brothers disenchanted with one another, but would pour his heart to bring peace between them. On one of his trips to France, he met a French Catholic Nun who was about to quit her Vow for Christ as a result of heavy pressure. Monk Peter encouraged her to embrace the sufferings of the Cross for the sake of loving Christ. Promising that he would join with his fellow Monks, back in Egypt, to pray for her that the Lord would give her Grace and Strength, the Nun returned to her monastic living, walking with the Lord in newness of life. He also led a French artist, who was an atheist, to The Lord. Later, the artist sent him a portrait of a Saint he saw in a Vision, which was that of St. Macarius the Great, the Patron Saint of Monk Peter's Monastery.

"As to his inner life, Monk Peter was glowing with the fire of the Spirit of Love. He would not stop singing while driving, repeating the words, 'We miss you so much, Lord Jesus; we desire so much to see you'. Through the Scriptures, which he memorized and treasured in his heart, he perfected prayer and praise. One day, he went to his Spiritual Father complaining that he had no time to pray. Father Mathew-the-Poor told him that he could make his day 48 hours instead of 24! 'How is this possible?', asked Peter. The Father answered: 'When you pray in the same hour you are asked to work, you double the time: one for work and the other for prayer'. Peter understood and perfected prayer while working, enjoying the permanent presence of The Lord in his inner monastic cell, or driving the truck, or speaking with others, or executing a task: for his heart was always overflowing with the Love of Christ.

"In the last days, before his departure, all evidence indicates that he knew that his time was near to be with the Lord he loved. He said goodby to so many, as if he was about to travel; and no one suspected that he was travelling to Heaven, because they were used to seeing him on frequent assignments outside the Monastery. Since he never complained of any physical ailment, many of his Monk Brothers were greatly shocked to know of his sudden departure. Father Mathew-the-Poor wrote the following on the day of his departure:

> *"In the monastic traditions, when eulogizing the life of a departed Monk who lived righteously and fulfilled his Monastic Vows, they say that: 'He poured water on the hands of the Saints'; and if the Monk deserved a higher esteem, they say: 'He washed the feet of the Saints'; but I say that 'Peter surpassed them all, because he even kissed their feet; for in the moments when Divine Light exploded in his heart, Peter completed The Lord's Commandment and snatched his Crown. He passed on and left for us The Lord's Example to emulate. Now he is deservedly graced by the praise of the One he loved.'"*

CHAPTER 2

A SUDDEN CALL TO GO

"I was drowsing off, about to sleep, when I heard an urgent knock at my door. I stepped out: a pleasant surprise was waiting for me. My hour at last had come. The Angel of Death appeared to whisk my Soul away to my eternal home! - and I recognized him at once. We glanced at each other fondly, and freely telepathized. Our thoughts were neatly locked in: words were a nuisance, and whispers were out of place.

"My immediate and burning desire was to record my journey. My Brothers, the Monks in the Monastery, would love to know how I arrived to Heaven. I thought of getting the Angel's permission first - a pen and pad would do. He managed a serious smile and nodded. He cautioned me, though, not to write any of the so-called Heavenly Mysteries which could not be explained in human terms, or described by earthly languages (2 Corinthians 12:4). They could not be understood, any way. I thanked him, however, for giving me this opportunity; and for accepting the intercessions of the Saints, on my behalf."

The Hour of Death

"Truly, the 'hour of death' is awesome and majestic. Wrapped in its unique mystique and wonder when it finally approached, it overwhelmed me utterly to the core. I must admit that I had been affectionately expecting it for some time; however, fear and apprehension gripped my heart when it suddenly arrived. All my preparation for this moment vanished, and I somehow seemed terribly inadequate.

"I could trace my feeble efforts, planning for this hour, to the time of my ordination as a Monk or maybe a little bit earlier, when I decided to leave the world behind. I may have died to the world as a Monk, but I really questioned if I was truly ready for Eternal Life. It was a one-way trip with no return. The intensity of the 'hour of death' is directly proportional to the state of the Soul at the time of its departure. The Soul is either conscious or unconscious, alert or saddled with all sorts of careless and neglectful baggage.

"To some who sincerely prepared themselves, dying to their egos through the Love of God, and for their fellow human-beings (1 Corinthians 1:7), this exodus was sheer joy and rapture: a time of merriment and celebration. As we read in the Bible and in the history of the Saints, godly people died experiencing a glow of light, reflected even on those around them. Some had their faces literally lit like the Sun. Others witnessed Angelic and Heavenly hosts calling them up. It has also been chronicled that some saw Heaven opened, and Jesus Himself stretching His Arms welcoming them from His Throne (Acts 7:56). Yet, to those who allowed themselves to ignore this moment, facing the inevitable would sweep them with an overwhelming avalanche of terror (Luke 17:20-37). The unprepared Soul would shake violently with horrifying anxiety, not knowing what hit it.

"As for myself, the happiness of my departure was mixed with the concerns of closing the Books, and paying down, somehow quickly, my outstanding debts (Luke 19:15)."

Two Great Opposing Powers:

"At the time of death, two great opposing powers do fiercely fight over the departing Soul. One is negative, cold, cruel and inhumane, drawing its power from the accumulative debts of unloving acts, guilt, lust for more, and the acquaintances of rutted friendships. The other power is positive, gentle and comforting: its strength being in acts of kindness, faith and goodness. The former drags the Soul down towards a deep gulf of despair, grief and hopelessness. The latter, on the other hand, pulls the Soul upward and charges it with joy, infusing it with tender love and potent hope. These two powers continue their relentless warfare until one of them wins the battle. This is my recollection of what happened to me after leaving the world behind."

The Robe

"I looked around in my cell and acknowledged my own body lying breathless. It was of a middle-aged, sleeping man; but soon it would be buried in the dust. Somehow, as a Monk, I managed avoiding looking at myself in the mirror; and honestly, I forgot what I really looked like. Still, I recognized my temple, the abode that I had dwelt in for forty years on Earth; but I knew that my body was not me.

"I also browsed quickly at whatever I had to carry with me on my journey. I found nothing worth taking (Ecclesiastes 1:14; 2:11). I examined the depth of my Soul, and was certain that money, power, position, physical beauty and praises were all worthless (1 Peter 1:24). In any event, I was not allowed to take anything with me, good or bad, except for a worn-out robe. The invisible tunic was old, as my age: only spirits could see it.

"The garment was initially as white as snow, but now was tarnished and shamefully stained. I put it on to cover my nakedness, and bolted towards the door. At this moment, I was in-between two worlds: the physical and the spiritual. The Angel of Death was quick to teach me my first lesson in the spirit-world. Apparently, my spirit did not need a door to get out! My departure would be like a shuttle lift-off from a visible to an invisible realm. For me, it was freedom from a dingy prison to the infinite cosmos of beauty."

CHAPTER 3

EXIT OF THE SPIRIT

"In an instant, I felt my spirit being unduly cramped, as if going out of a tiny bottleneck to an extraterrestrial existence. It touched the first step into the New World without landing, a world that had no resemblance to the old. Time and space were history. I looked down, and I could see the whole-inhabited Planet Earth like a drop in a great ocean: like a tiny seed in the hand of the Great Creator.

"My body was still lying on the ground, in the dust from which it had come (Genesis 3:19). At the time of my departure, I saw another spirit departing from another place on this tiny drop, which we call the Globe. So, I had a companion headed with me to the final destination."

Reactions To My Death

"I felt no hurry to leave at once. I thought of checking a few things first. I was curious to read the faces of my past acquaintances, relatives in the flesh, Brothers in the Lord - and see their reaction to my death. I wanted to find out the inner feelings of both friends and enemies alike. (A Monk has an enemy? You would be surprised! Truly, I had no enemies; but sadly, few hid their animosity against me deep in their hearts).

"**The first** was my best friend among the Brothers. He was weeping and deeply shaken. His mannerism revealed the symptoms of a near-sighted spirit. The poor fellow was aching and loathing missing me. Somehow, he might have felt that I betrayed him, leaving him behind. I smiled, tried to sooth him gently to comfort his broken heart; but he could not even feel me. I forgot that his eyes were held shut.

"Others gathered around my deceased body, either with the numbness of shock and disbelief, or with callousness of heart. They gathered also to console my closest friend, who was utterly devastated. Among the group, a child-like Brother was busy pouring his heart, supporting my friend. His consoling words had such balmy power on a bleeding heart. The Holy Spirit gently and artfully orchestrated his words to its most-needed destination.

"Some in the group were exchanging sterile words of condolences. Motivated only by obligation, their hearts were distant and cold. They could not share any true sympathy, and their mumbling returned back to them empty. Sadly, they were like clouds without rain, and autumn trees without fruit.

"**The second** was also weeping, but his tears were different! I saw him rushing to his closet with a halo around his head. I understood that the halo was the enlightenment. He offered sweet worshipping and repentance. It appeared that my death rekindled the Vows for the cleansing and washing of his Soul.

"**The third** was uniquely special. He was in a state of immaculate joy. With such a trusting eye of the supremacy of the life to come, he immediately shared with Heaven its joys. How sweet was his selfless labor of love toward me, while I was still on Earth. How great was his future crown.

"**The fourth** was oddly different. He seemed nonchalant, with a touch of relief. His heart was smudged with a dark secret, and depression marred his countenance. He was choked with competition over an earthly position. Tragically, he was envious of a Gift that was entrusted only to me.

"The unfortunate fifth was not only lukewarm but spiritually dead. My departure did not move him or even dent his Soul. He was content with earthly, religious responsibilities and endless greed for more."

Time To Go

"At this point, the Angel of Death yanked me saying: 'That is it! You've seen enough! This must be left behind at once. You must get ready for what is ahead. You are about to face the ultimate litmus test that is so horrific for humans to overcome.'

"Sheepishly, I turned around and was startled by a group of demons; they were standing with piercing eyes, looking straight at me. They were very ugly, and had a giant chief whose beard was crooked as if untimely plucked, and an arrow had penetrated his heart. Nervously awaiting my Passover and anxious of its outcome, he was standing in great apprehension.

"On the other side, there was a group of bright Angels, their faces so soft and gentle, but their natures were of blazing fire. Only by melodious praises and songs, sweet and tender, were they spreading peace to hearts. They also had a Chief, with whom I had an immediate affinity. Somehow, I felt that my relationship with this particular Archangel was not recent; and I could not remember exactly when our friendship started or blossomed. It was assuring to see that the group of Angels was larger than that of the demons (4 Kingdoms 6:16), and that the Angels had trusting, quiet expectation in support of me."

The Accusations

"The demons did not waste time. They immediately started whispering; and with murmuring, accusative looks, pointed at my stained robe. I studied them and their armour, and recognized numerous land-mines and traps. I was even able to remember some of their faces. Sadly, I got acquainted with a few while on Earth. I gullibly and intimately befriended the demons without telling my Spiritual Father and Counselor. Acknowledging pride, lying, theft, fornication, judgment and others, I was able to quickly discern most of them.

"I wanted to see what they were pointing at, and was horrified to find that every stain on my robe carried a picture of one of these demons. I understood what it meant: they had a part of me, and were claiming it back. Their evidence was the seal of their ugly faces stuck on my robe. Utterly speechless, I felt that I needed an advocate.

"I went to my friend, the Archangel, for advice about the chief demon: what he was up to. Gently, he identified the chief demon as the one appointed for my fall and ultimate destruction by using his gang and their wily armour of booby traps. Immediately, I felt great dislike towards them. I was sure that this feeling was not recent; rather, it started way back when I renounced satan and all his troops during my Baptism as a child.

"I did inquire about the dagger piercing the chief-demon's heart. The Archangel affirmed that it was my form of Monkhood. At once, the Holy Spirit revealed a flashback of that glorious day when the Monks prayed over me, and dressed me in the 'eskim' or the form of Monkhood. I saw the same chief-demon gravely angry, gnashing his teeth and plucking his beard. Vehemently, he was threatening, cursing and cussing with disgusting, profane language. For a short moment, I felt sorry for his poor state; and I sincerely hoped that he might have a chance to repent. Somehow, I understood and rationalized his anger."

Critical Stage

"Once again, I returned to the scene, asking my Guardian Angel about the demons that I could not recognize. My Angel Friend reminded me of the times when I blocked my ears against their voices, based on counsel from the Holy Spirit and His Angels. At other times, when I listened to the demons but immediately offered sincere repentance, the Lord kindly wiped out both their image and remembrance from my robe - and my memory as well.

"I looked at my Friends, the Angels, asking for peace in this grave and difficult moment. They were all full of tender love, gentleness and humility. Each one had, in one hand, a bouquet of the good fruits that belonged to the Holy Spirit. Apparently, the Spirit was always encouraging me to receive them. In their other hand, they carried a mighty Sword, the **Word of God** (Ephesians 6:17), to destroy the armies of demons, the angels of darkness and evil.

"The Angel of Death Emerged and marched along sounding the Trumpet. An Eastern Door suddenly appeared before my eyes, leading to an extraordinary, bright place. Although I could not see exactly what was behind, I was definitely anxious to be inside. I eyed also, at the opposite end, a slope leading to a deep, bottomless pit which was abhorrently dark; and the scene frightened me immensely.

"I darted away, forcing myself with all my might, and insisting to enter the Eastern Door. As soon as I got closer, two Angel Guards stopped me. I smiled at them, thinking that they were asking for a visa or a passport, but they too pointed to the stains on my robe. Though they were not accusative like the demons, they were firm. They repeated to me the verse: 'Those who do such things . . . **cannot** inherit the kingdom of God' (Galatians 5:21). I had a debt to be paid; and my accusers, the demons, had every right to take me with them!!!"

The Door Is Closed

"Immediately, a huge magnet sucked me toward the Western Gate. I cried for help. There was none! My Archangel Friend explained that it was only natural and inevitable to happen. The stains on my robe were drawn entirely to their origin and source, taking me all the way to Hell. There was no way to erase them, because the time of repentance had already passed. To my surprise, I found my death companion was also drawn with me to the abyss, albeit with fewer spots than mine.

"In the last seconds, just before landing in the depth of darkness, I cried out:

'Where is the Christ of my Salvation?!'

I honestly regretted, deeply, everything I had done that caused staining my robe and ruining my chances to be with my Lord. At this moment, there was no single creature, an Angel or a Saint, capable of rescuing me. The demons' smirking faces smelt of imminent victory as both my death companion and I were descending helplessly, sobbing and wailing."

CHAPTER 4

THE LAMB OF GOD

"Suddenly, a great Light swiftly shocked the foundation of darkness. A blazing Being and a majestic Royalty stood with indescribable beauty, surrounded by millions of his Angels. I knew Him at once:

'JESUS!!!'

I knelt down, lifting my eyes and begging him for mercy – not by uttering a single word, but only by pleading looks. I recognized Him instantly and loved Him. Although I had not seen Him before (1 Peter 1:8), I had tasted him, often experiencing His Grace and Kindness.

"His Image was always imprinted on my heart. Incredibly, I discovered that I looked like him. His Own Seal was marked on my face (Galatians 6:17), which Image I received the day He bore me. As for the stains on my robe, they were the result of the accumulative hardness of my heart over the span of my brief life."

I Saw Jesus

"This is my Bridegroom, the most beautiful among all people: The One, Whom my heart desires, and in Him my hope rests (Song of Songs 5:16). I have waited all my life for this moment, also seeing it with the intense eyes of Hope. This is the One whom I believed in and leaned on. He never left me for a moment, or even for a twinkle of an eye. To him, I submitted my whole life. This is my Beloved; I repeatedly called Him, and He always answered me. Singing to Him, His name was sweeter than honey in my mouth. He is the Hope of nations, and the Salvation of all peoples.

> *'For the Scripture says, "Whoever believes on Him will not be put to shame."' *(Romans10:11); and*

> *'As it is written: "Behold, I lay in Zion a stumbling stone and rock of offence, and whoever believes on Him will not be put to shame."' *(Romans 9:33).*

"I was certain of His Presence, and sure of his deliverance for, as soon as Jesus put His Arms around me (Song of Songs 8:3), I saw the nailed Hands and the pierced Side bleeding profusely afresh. I was so puzzled and amazed to see that our Spring of Salvation is still gushing. One drop of His oozing, Divine Blood was more than adequate to cleanse me entirely from all my sins (Ephesians 1:7), and make my stained robe whiter than snow (1 Corinthians 15:52).

> *'But thanks be to God, who gives us the victory through Our Lord Jesus Christ.' *(1 Corinthians 15:57)"*

Sad Ending

"Suddenly, I heard an agonizing cry. It was by the chief demon and his gang. They were wailing, falling hard to the bottomless pit, and chained to the darkness of Hell. (2 Peter 2:4) Because of their dark state, they were sucked into their eternal gloom by the natural order. They could neither stay in the Light, nor have any fellowship with God (2 Corinthians 6:14).

"I searched for my death companion, and found him still wearing his stained robe, sinking quickly to Hell. I shouted, *'Look, this is Jesus; call upon him'*; but sadly, he could not understand what I meant. I was dumbfounded that he did not have a clue of the source of Salvation: he did not feel or believe in Jesus (Hebrews 3:19). I understood that he had neither the Image of the Redeemer nor the time to get to know Him. My death companion took the final plunge with such painful moaning. I felt so bad for him, and wished that he had known what I was privileged to hear and see (Mark 16:16, John 8:24).

"Noticing The Lord looking at me, I felt awkwardly embarrassed. My dress was not appropriate to meet Him. I was so ashamed of myself (1 John 2:28); but the Lord, my Beloved, knew my thoughts, and immediately dressed me with a Robe shinier than the Sun (1 Corinthians 15:49, Philippians 3:21, and Colossians 3:10), made of His Righteousness, and of the Holiness of His Truth (Ephesians 4:24). Immediately, a few of its threads started to glow."

Mysteries of Heaven

"I relaxed like a baby in Jesus' Arms, tucked comfortably in His Bosom. I then understood the meaning of the Scripture:

> *'. . . Eye has not seen, nor ear heard, nor have entered into the heart of man the things which God has prepared for those who love Him.' *(1 Corinthians 2:9).*

The Eastern Gate was opened, and the songs of victory pouring in were an extraordinary flow of vibrant melodies of triumph: Angels' praises peppered with harmonies of the Saints' sweet and moving chanting had such an intoxicating aroma of pure prayers. I wanted to write down what I saw, heard, felt and smelled; but realized that the language of man could not describe this awesome glory.

"Fixated at the vividly-bleeding puncture on my Beloved's side, a New Life sprung up within me: my whole mind, feelings, senses and understanding had changed. Hidden mysteries were revealed, and indescribable glories became suddenly known to me (2 Corinthians 3:18)."

The Secret behind the Glimmer of the Threads of the Robe

"Among what I understood, was the secret behind the shining threads in my Robe. By the Grace of God, some of my deeds, though few in number, were matching his Divine Purpose. I had put on the Sufferings of Christ (1 John 3:2). His Glory, indeed, reflected on every painful experience or fiery trial I had endured for Him (2 Peter 1:4).

"I saw around me a group of Saints (Colossians 1:12; 1 Thessalonians 3:13), and I recognized them one by one, even though they had one Image and one appearance (Romans 8:29). Also, I noticed that my Image and appearance were similar to theirs (2 Corinthians 3:18). Every one of them also was wearing a shining Robe; but the level of shimmering differed and varied (1 Corinthians 15:41)."

The Blessed Virgin Mary

"On the Right Hand of the Lord Jesus (Psalm 45:9) was a distinguished, beautiful and gentle Lady. Her whole Robe shone brilliantly, woven with gold (Psalm 45:13), as Her Life had been so fitting and so full of harmony with The Divine Will. The Lord was pleased to dwell in Her, and made Her radiance far superior to any other human being or Angelic Creature.

"The tenderness of her Motherhood was evident as she offered Her Robe to anyone asking for her prayers; however, the Robe stayed on her with dazzling shimmer. I witnessed those who were still on Earth, interceding for the Virgin's help. They too stood before The Lord with the Robe of the Righteousness of Christ, the very One that belonged to Mary. She was indeed the Mother of the Son of God.

"I also saw the Saints who have been crowned. They too imitated the Virgin Mary, and took off their Robes to clothe whoever asked, as an amicable gesture of fellowship and love. Although the traps of the devil could not overcome those who wore them, that did not prevent the envious devils from repeating their attacks.

"Among a group of exquisite achievers, with brilliant Crowns on their heads, I was able to recognize the great Heroes: St. George, St. Demiana and many others, whose stories I had not heard while on Earth; but they were well-known in Heaven. I could identify them immediately, as if I had lived with them all along. A wonderful fragrance eminated from them: the scent of the blood they had shed in the Name of Christ, and for which they received their Crowns of Martyrdom."

The Loving and the Confessors

"Another distinct group, I named the 'Lovely or the Loving', were not Martyrs, Apostles or Prophets; but were ordinary people full of tender love. Each praised, playing with a harp (Revelation 5:8; 15:2). They rejoiced, not only for being in the presence of the Beloved forever, but also for being **in** Him (Galatians 2:20).

"A fourth group had very shiny-bodied members: some had radiant stomachs due to an ascetic life; some had blazing heads since they had found no place to rest them; some had luminous feet, for they wandered in deserts and wastelands, poor and preaching the Good News of the Kingdom; others were tortured, not accepting deliverance, so that they might obtain a better resurrection (Hebrews 11:35); they were rewarded for their sufferings with Glory, and a great glow seared their tortured members."

Inheriting the Kingdom

"There were also Angels who specialized in serving those who inherit Salvation (Hebrews 1:14). One of them approached me, and seated me at the end of all the rows. My Robe shone the least of all; however, in truth, I was extremely happy and content, because I could not see myself worthy to be in that place. I neither deserved beholding my Beloved Lord, nor joining the Heavenly Choir in their exquisite, harmonious praise."

CHAPTER 5

BACK TO EARTH

"I awoke, and looked around to find that I had not yet completed my earthly struggle. Alas, I was still in the body; but my desire and my longing for Heaven had been rekindled and sparked with Hope. Determined to wash my Robe in the Blood of the Lamb at once, I wanted to be ready for my final encounter with my Lord. Now, I also had a heightened awareness of, and attention to, that awesome Passover!"

"May the Lord have mercy on us, and give us deliverance on the day of Judgment! Everlasting glory, praise, thanks and honor are due to Him forever."

"Amen!"

www.ingramcontent.com/pod-product-compliance
Lightning Source LLC
Chambersburg PA
CBHW031253120626
46545CB00007B/2798